BJ's Adventures:
National Symbols

Author : Tomiko Cobb   Illustrator : Ika Wahyu

Library of Congress Catalog Card Number:2024903561

ISBN: 979-8-9894025-2-6 (hardcover)

Publishing Dreams Agency, LLC.
Snellville, Georgia 30039

www.educatedbookworms.com

I0096534

Hi! My name is BJ! Have you ever wondered what your national symbols look like?
Do you want to help me find them?
Come along as we go on the next BJ's Adventure to search for National Symbols!

What is a symbol?
The United States has many symbols.
A symbol is something that stands or
represent for something else.
For example,
A heart is a symbol for love. A dove is a
symbol for peace.

Gold Dollar

Half Dollar

Silver Dollar

Quarter Dollar

BALD EAGLE

The Bald Eagle was chosen on June 20, 1782 as an emblem of the United States of America. The Bald Eagle has been a symbol of the United States since 1782.

Bald Eagle represents strength and bravery (freedom). Can spread wings 7 feet wide.

Bald eagles are not bald, they have white feathers on its head. You can find a Bald Eagle on the backs of American gold coins, silver dollar, half dollar, and quarter.

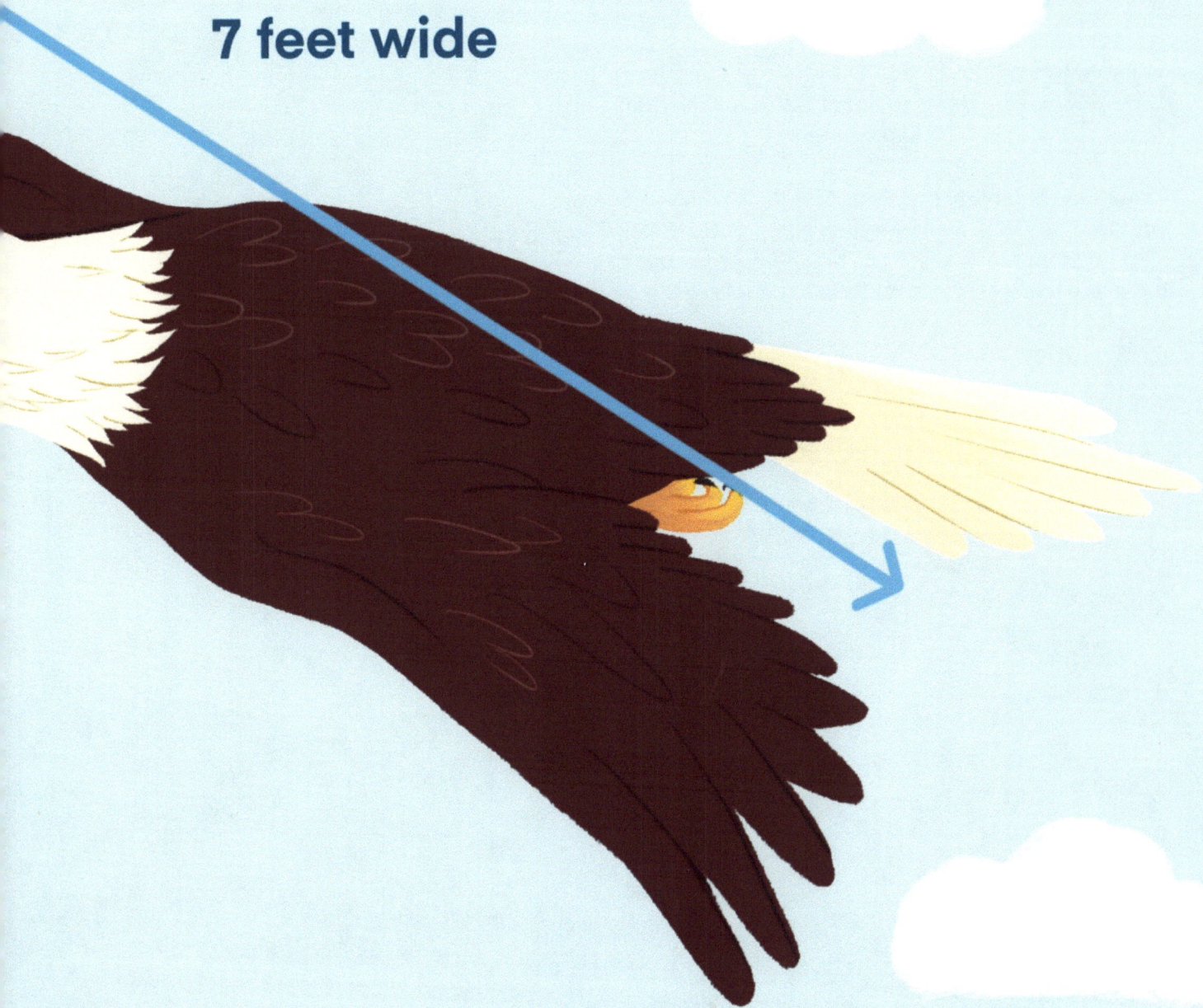

7 feet wide

STATUE OF LIBERTY

The statue was a gift to United States from the people of France. Lady Liberty was meant to honor the friendship between the two countries.

The Statue of Liberty stands on Liberty Island, just off the southern tip of Manhattan Island, a part of New York City. The statue is about 151 feet (46 meters) tall. The statue has welcomed millions of people to the country.

151 feet
(46 meters)

LINCOLN MEMORIAL

The Lincoln Memorial is a monument dedicated to Abraham Lincoln, the 16th president of the United States. Inside the memorial is a marble statue of Lincoln seated in a chair. The statue is 19 feet (5.8 meters) tall.

The Lincoln Memorial was an important symbol for the American civil rights movement. In 1963 Martin Luther King, Jr., delivered his famous "I Have a Dream" speech from the steps of the Lincoln Memorial.

WASHINGTON MONUMENT

The Washington Monument is a building honoring George Washington, the first president of the United States. It is located in Washington, D.C.

Built to honor George Washington. He helped the United States become a country and was the 1st President. The monument is just under 555 feet (169 meters) tall. The Washington Monument was opened to visitors on October 9, 1888.

Inside the monument, an elevator can take visitors to an observation deck at the top in 60 seconds. Visitors can take the elevator back down or walk the more than 800 steps.

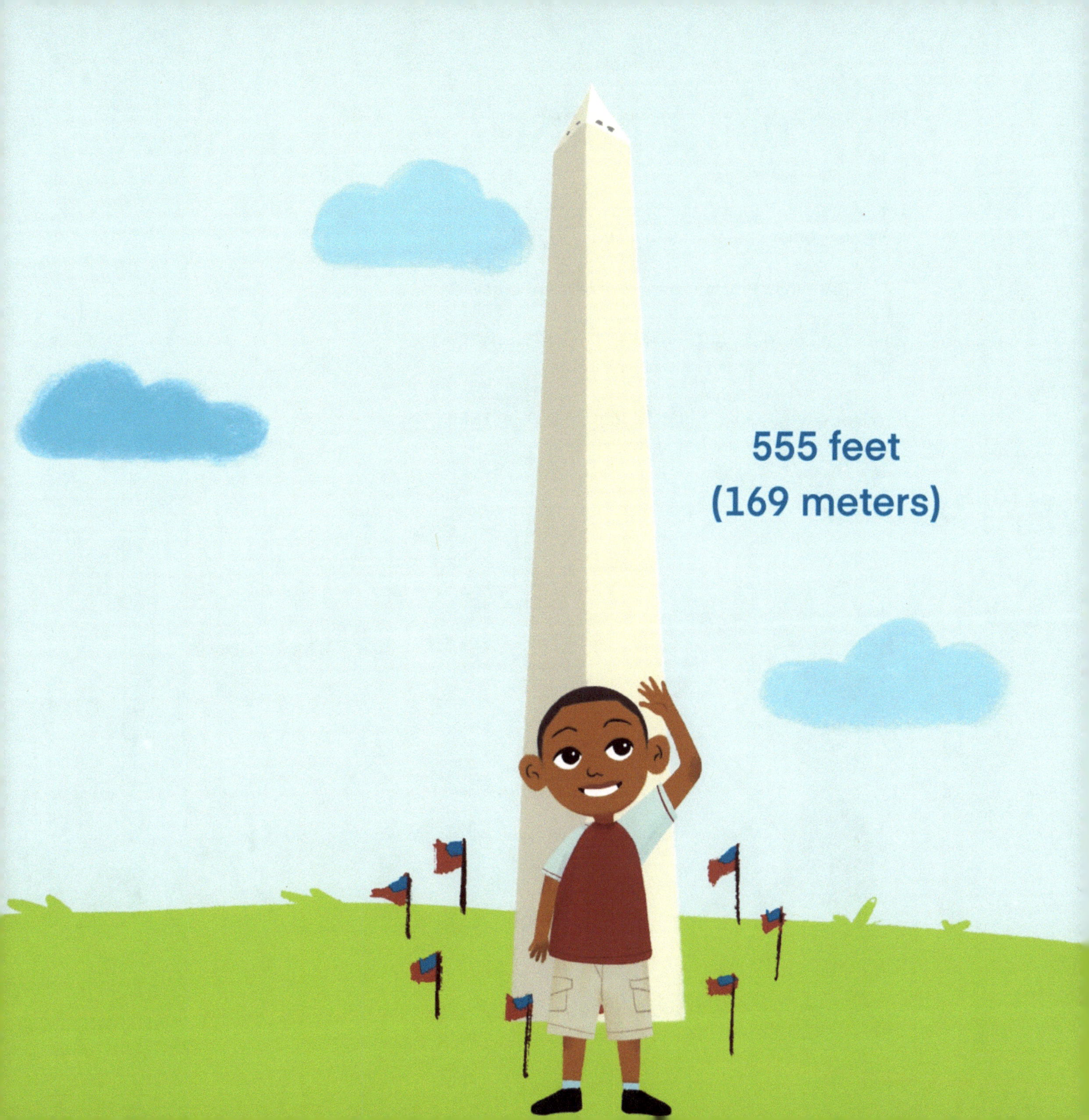

555 feet
(169 meters)

WHITE HOUSE

The president of the United States lives and works in the White House. The president's family lives there also.

The White House is a symbol of democracy.

United States Presidents have lived in and worked in the White House since 1800.

The White House is in Washington, D.C., at 1600 Pennsylvania Avenue N.W.

UNITED STATES FLAG

The national flag of the United States of America is a
patriotic symbol for Americans all over the world.

Every school day millions of American schoolchildren
recite the Pledge of Allegiance to the flag.

The flag is a symbol of the United States. Its colors are red, white, and blue.
White stands for purity.
Red means strength.
Blue stands for justice.

The U.S. Flag has 50 stars. There is one star for each
state in the nation.

Flag's 13 stripes stand for 13 original colonies that
become a state.

**13 Stripe original
colonies**

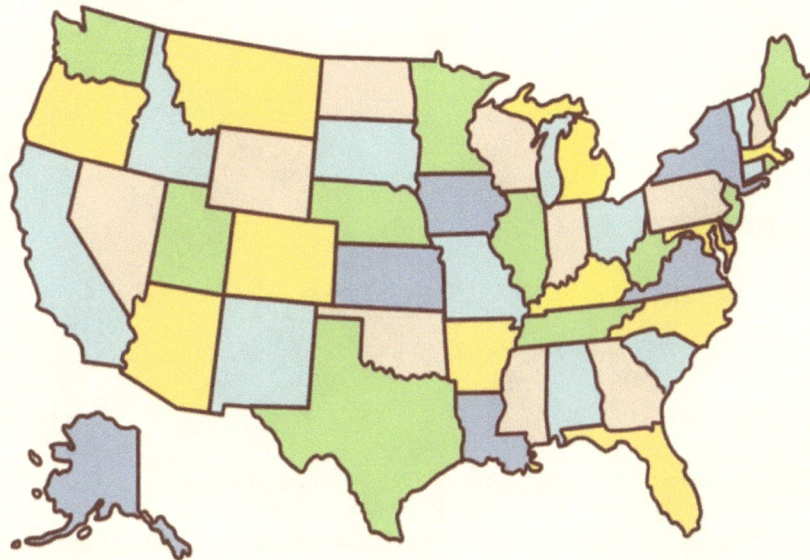

**50 Stars for
each states**

PLEDGE OF ALLEGIANCE

People pledge allegiance to the flag of the United States to show devotion and respect for their country.

People recite the pledge of allegiance at public gatherings and ceremonies. In many schools, students and teachers recite the pledge of allegiance before classwork begins. While reciting, people stand and remove their hats as a sign of respect for the country. People place their right hand over their heart and say these words together:

I pledge allegiance to the flag of the United States of America and to the republic for which it stands, one nation under God, indivisible, with liberty and justice for all.

STAR SPANGLE BANNER

"The Star-Spangled Banner" is the official national
anthem of the United States.
Star Spangled Banner is sung at sports events.

This song is a symbol of American Patriotism.

The song has 4 stanzas but only the first one is usually sung:

O say, can you see, by the dawn's early light,
What so proudly we hailed at the twilight's last gleaming,
Whose broad stripes and bright stars, through the perilous fight,

O'er the ramparts we watched, were so gallantly streaming?
And the rockets' red glare, the bombs bursting in air,
Gave proof through the night that our flag was still there;

O say, does that star-spangled banner yet wave

O'er the land of the free and the home of the brave?

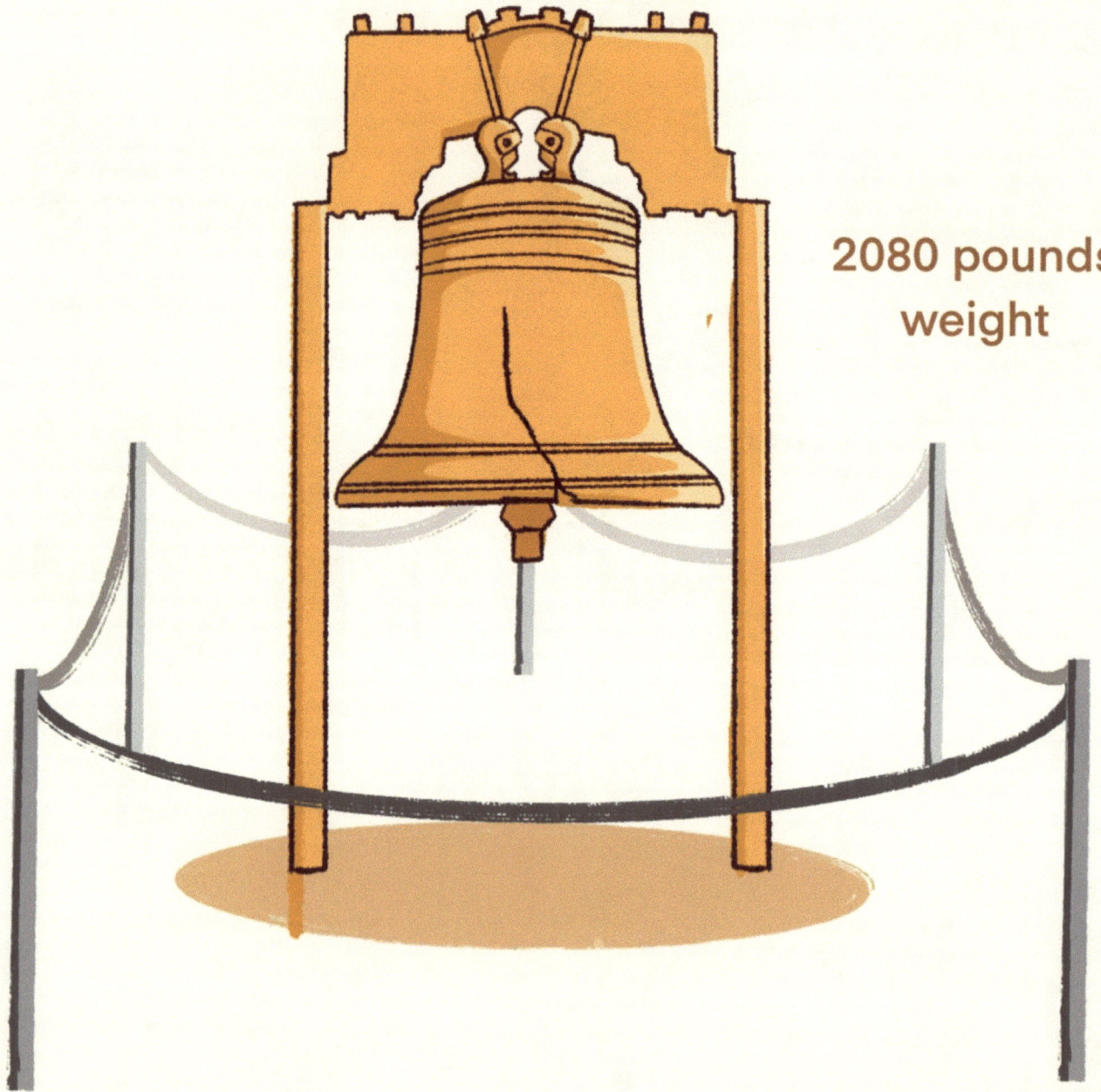

2080 pounds
weight

LIBERTY BELL

The Liberty Bell is in Philadelphia, Pennsylvania.
It's called the State House Bell or Old State House Bell.

It was made in 1752 for the Pennsylvania State House.
The Liberty Bell is a symbol of freedom and independence.

The Liberty Bell is 2,080 pounds in weight.
The Bell is three feet tall from lip to crown.

The lip's circumference is 12 feet long,
while the crown's circumference is 6 feet, 11 inches long.

Today that building is called Independence Hall.

Pennysilvania
State House

Questions

Why do we use symbols?

What are some symbols of the United States?

Where do we see and use these symbols?

Why do we use them in specific places and at specific times?

Why do groups of people use symbols?

How does a group pick its symbols?

How does a symbol help a group come together?

What groups and symbols do you see in
your school or community?

Vocabulary

Symbol

Colonies

Patriotism

Extinct

Harbor

Monument

The End

www.ingramcontent.com/pod-product-compliance
Lightning Source LLC
Chambersburg PA
CBHW061147030426

42335CB00002B/136